John Birks "Dizzy" Gillespie

Gillespie

A Man, a Trumpet, and a Journey to Bebop

John Birks "Dizzy" Gillespie
A Man, a Trumpet, and a Journey to Bebop

by Susan Engle

illustrated by Luthando Mazibuko

BELLWOOD PRESS

WILMETTE, ILLINOIS

Bellwood Press, Wilmette, Illinois
401 Greenleaf Ave, Wilmette, Illinois 60091
Copyright © 2019 by Susan Engle
All rights reserved. Published 2019
Printed in the United States of America ∞

22 21 20 19   1 2 3 4

Library of Congress Cataloging in Publication Data

Names: Engle, Susan, author.
Title: John Birks "Dizzy" Gillespie : a man, a trumpet, and a journey
    to bebop / Susan Engle.
Description: Wilmette : Bellwood Press, 2019. | Series: Change maker
    |
  Includes bibliographical references. | Audience: Ages 11–15 |
    Audience:
  Grades 7–9
Identifiers: LCCN 2019040949 (print) | LCCN 2019040950 (ebook)
    | ISBN
  9781618511539 (paperback) | ISBN 9781618511553 (ebook)
Subjects: LCSH: Gillespie, Dizzy, 1917–1993—Juvenile literature. |
    Jazz
  Musicians—United States—Biography—Juvenile literature. |
    Trumpet
  players—United States—Biography—Juvenile literature.
Classification: LCC ML3930.G47 E65 2019 (print) | LCC ML3930.
    G47 (ebook)
  | DDC 788.9/2165092 [B]—dc23
LC record available at https://lccn.loc.gov/2019040949
LC ebook record available at https://lccn.loc.gov/2019040950

Cover art and illustrations by Luthando Mazibuko, copyright ©
by the National Spiritual Assembly of the Bahá'ís of the United States
Book design by Patrick Falso

For those who, like Dizzy,
have generously showered their musical gifts upon all alike,
regardless of the color of the listener's skin.

Contents

Acknowledgments

Dizzy Gillespie's life reminded me of a tornado. He was so busy playing trumpet and learning new skills that he was in constant motion and only seemed to stop whirling to sleep when it was absolutely necessary. Happily, you can get a visual taste of his personality and energy—a list of some of my favorite videos of him performing can be viewed later in the book.

As I continue to learn and write about the lives of African Americans who were "Change Makers" and made a positive impact on our society, I am grateful for the women and men who have voluntarily shared their strength and vulnerability and have educated me and other white people about what it is like to wake up black in the United States. No one has the right to ask for the generosity of spirit I've been shown from black friends, neighbors, and educators. I appreciate the toll this emotional labor can exact and have learned so much from their experiences.

My daughters Layli Phillips and Bahiyyih Baker have faithfully served as first readers and editors, and they continue to offer encouragement to me along the way. I am grateful for the work of Christopher

Martin of Bellwood Press, who shares his editorial skills so patiently and thoroughly.

I will always be thankful to Bonnie Taylor for directing me down the path to writing biographies of heroes for kids. There are many treasures to find in the lives of people who published ground-breaking newspapers, pioneered the art of jazz, created moving poetry, and inspired others in ways that changed the world for the better. My hope is that readers of this book will find a whirlwind of inspiration to develop their own talents and to help shape a peaceful future for our planet.

Introduction

He just couldn't sit still. Usually, this was because there was music going on in the room or in his head. But today, he was getting ready to make a trip to two big cities up north. Tomorrow, he, his brothers, and his mother would all get on the train. His father had saved enough money for part of the family to travel. Despite his restlessness, the young boy couldn't stop smiling.

The smell of chicken frying, along with bread and pie baking, didn't calm him one bit. He knew that taking home-cooked food was important on such a long trip. The train was divided between cars for white people and cars for black people, and good food wasn't provided for the second group. The boy had been told that even if he got lucky, he would only find some dried-up old ham sandwiches. Never mind. He wouldn't get better tasting food than the yummy goodies that his friends and family were helping prepare in the kitchen.[1]

All the talk and laughter made him think of his grandpa, Paw, who lived in his own little house at the end of the yard. Paw knew how to make people laugh. He would tell a funny story, and as he went along, his voice would become louder and louder and louder. When he delivered the punchline, he looked as if he were shouting, but his voice was only a whisper. Every time, friends and family who had gathered around and were listening to Paw would double over with laughter. The boy absolutely loved Paw's comedy, and he had decided to work on being funny along with playing the music that was constantly jumping around in his brain.[2] Tomorrow, at the end of the train ride, when he could tune in to some radio stations, he was going to listen to some jazz. That music felt as alive as he was and always inspired him.

He was going to spend a whole summer in Philadelphia and New York! The population of his hometown of Cheraw, South Carolina, was small—only about three thousand five hundred people were living there when he was born.[3] Unfortunately, racism was alive and well in Cheraw. White people treated black people as if the days of slavery had never ended. Someone who was black didn't deserve to be thought of

as a human being by whites—at least, this is how the boy had felt in his hometown as he grew up.[4] He had often wondered if things were even a little different up north.

Well, he was now eight years old, and he was about to see for himself. The long days of preparation for the journey finally came to an end. At the station, the

train made all of its exciting loud noises and squealed to a stop. It was hard for an excited boy to stay far enough away from the tracks to keep from getting crushed by the huge wheels. He managed to climb aboard with a happy heart and all his limbs intact. Half of his family was off to stay awhile with his Aunt Rose and Uncle Henry!

The visit was wonderful. His aunt often left extra fruit on the kitchen table for him and his brothers, and she and her husband took the family by trolley to a picnic—a big picnic with free ice cream. He tried every flavor—twelve or thirteen in all, and he would always remember that the person serving up the scoops was white. This friendly fellow smiled at all the people who came by, regardless of their skin color. Just as amazingly, all the children—black and white alike—were playing baseball and laughing together.[5]

So it was true—there was a little bit of paradise up north. He would never forget this experience. When he was old enough and the time was right, he was determined to head away from his hometown and never look back. He could hardly wait.

1. Where the Music Began

John Birks Gillespie's parents had a total of eleven children.[6] Two children in the family had passed away as babies; they just didn't live "long enough to get a name."[7] The oldest, Sonny, left home when John was about five. Two other brothers fled to escape Papa Gillespie's temper. That left six children—three sisters and two brothers plus John, who was the youngest—to fill up the house during the years when John was going to school.

Mama Gillespie, whose name was Lottie, was warm and loving in her approach to raising children.[8] She was only fifteen when her oldest child was born, so she had to start thinking about motherhood when she was barely more than a child herself.[9] Perhaps that gave her lots of empathy for her little ones, whom she cared for at home for so many years.

Papa Gillespie was a hard worker. He was a bricklayer during the week and a piano player in a band on the weekends.[10] Even though he had many children to feed, John's father usually had enough money to put some food into the family's stomachs. When he did have a little extra income, he liked to buy expensive surprise gifts for Lottie. He would also occasionally come home from work with the pockets of his overalls full of candy. As his children scrambled over him searching for the sweets, he would laugh out loud.[11]

Even though Papa had kind moments, he also had a lot of pent-up anger inside him. He "roared when he talked,"[12] and John was afraid of him. Every Sunday, Papa Gillespie whipped his boys. He was always sure they had done *something* wrong during the week, and this was his way of making sure that the boys didn't get away with anything he might not have heard about. Sometimes John wondered if these regular whippings actually drove him to get into trouble. Whatever his reasoning, Papa always handed out the same weekly punishment to his sons, and these whippings instilled fear and anger in John.[13]

In spite of his fear of his father, John remembered the joy of handling Papa's musical instruments that were stored in the house during the week: a guitar, a mandolin, a clarinet, a big bass violin with only one string, a drum set, and a piano.[14] John had plenty of opportunities to play, to listen, and to learn how to make sounds on them all. He especially loved the drums and the piano, which he played with two fingers as a young child.

He worked out a tune when he was four years old and would bang it out on the keys that he could barely reach.

He would often run next door to his neighbor, Mrs. Harrington, and play for her on her piano as well. This was a treat for both of them. Mrs. Harrington's husband sold ice cream in his shoe shop, and she had lots of it on hand at home, so she would give John a bowl whenever he came running in. After playing a song for her over and over, John would dash back home and try out the song's rhythm on the drums for a while. His trips to his neighbor and back, and the switching from piano to drums to piano, could go on all day long. Mrs. Harrington soon recognized John's intelligence and began an impromptu preschool for him. She taught him the alphabet, how to count to one hundred, and how to read.[15]

By the time John was five, he was more than ready to go to school. In Cheraw, there was a school for white children that was separate from the school for black children. John's school was named after an African-American man named Robert Smalls. Mr. Smalls was a hero to the black community because he had helped other enslaved people escape to the North during the Civil War. During the brief time when black people could vote in the South after that war, Mr. Smalls was elected to Congress and stood up for the rights of African Americans. John would learn all of this history when he was closer to age forty than age four, but he was grateful when he eventually discovered the truth about his school's name.[16]

Thanks to Mrs. Harrington, John already knew the lessons that were being taught in his class, and as a result, he was often bored. He would whistle during class, and his teacher would always become angry. On his very first day, she made him come to the front of the class, and she beat his legs with a thin branch called a switch. When John's father heard about this, he immediately ran to the principal's house and told him that the teacher had "better not touch him no more!"[17] Seeing that his papa whipped him every Sunday, John was surprised that his father defended him from the very same treatment in the schoolroom. Apparently, Papa Gillespie thought that only he could whip his boys, but John never forgot how his father had jumped to his defense.

Because of his early lessons with Mrs. Harrington, John was soon promoted to the next grade. This promotion didn't cure his mischievous nature, though. During his school days in the 1920s, inkwells were placed on children's desks, and the kids would dip their pens into the inkwells whenever they were writing. John would fill these inkwells with "all sorts of stuff." He wrote, "[I would] mash chewing gum into the hair of every girl that I could lay my hands on, and was so mean they thought I was going to be a gangster. The teacher . . . beat me until I threatened to tell my mother, then she'd stop whipping me and put me in a dark closet. . . . I was terrified of that closet and could see all sorts of things . . . but I passed the first grade without getting killed."[18]

John needed an outlet for his energy. He spent a lot of time running, jumping, exploring, fighting, and freely playing his father's musical instruments. It wouldn't be long before he would be able to channel that energy into learning to master the trumpet. This passion would change his life.

2. Dark Days

In June of 1927, John Birks was nine years old.[19] It was very early in the morning when someone spotted a rabid dog in the Gillespie's yard. Papa Gillespie called in a neighbor to make sure the dog didn't bite anyone. It was sad that the dog had to be shot outside the house, but things were about to get worse. For no apparent reason, John's father suddenly began to have an asthma attack and couldn't breathe. John and his mother were able to get Papa Gillespie into the house and into bed.

John left the bedroom, but before long, he heard his mother start to cry. As hard as it was to believe, John knew then that his father had died.[20] The only positive thing he remembered about that day in June was finding the strap his father had used for his Sunday whippings and cutting it into little pieces.[21]

Papa Gillespie had worked two jobs to give the family a home, food, and clothing, and John's mother now had to make do with little jobs in town—such as washing clothes—for $1.50 to $2.00 a week.[22] These jobs didn't even begin to match Papa Gillespie's earnings. Money became tight, and new clothes were out of the question. In Cheraw, it was traditional for everyone to have new clothes for Easter. After Papa Gillespie's passing, however, whenever Easter morning came around, John and his brother Wesley would pack some lunch and head out to the woods for the day so that their friends and neighbors would not see that they had no new clothes to wear.[23]

The bad news didn't end with Papa Gillespie's death. A few months later, the president of the bank where the family kept their money ran away with all the family's savings.[24] The Gillespie family was now desperately poor.

The boys helped all they could. Though picking cotton was grueling work, Wesley was good at it. Whenever he was able to find work in the cotton fields, he gave his small earnings to his mother for the family's meals. John was not particularly good at this job. In fact, he hated it, so he decided to do other things to help out. Although Cheraw had separate pools for blacks and whites, John learned and practiced diving.

Soon he could do one and a half gainers (backward somersaults) and other tricks in the air. He was so good that the white pool management would hire him to come and show off his diving moves, and white folks would toss money into the pool for John to pick up from the bottom at the end of a dive.

John was also a good dancer. White people would invite him to parties to show off his signature "snake hips" dance, and they would throw money on the floor for him as payment. Sometimes John's diving and dancing would bring in $2.00 or $3.00 at a time. He did odd jobs, too, such as mowing lawns. This work usually added only fifteen cents to the household money, but like Wesley, John used his abundant energy to help his mother.

John's favorite job of all was working as a volunteer at the local movie theater. He had learned to sneak in to movies so effectively that the owner of the theater, after initially throwing him out several times, offered him a job to make sure other kids couldn't sneak in as well.[25] Even though the job paid him nothing, it offered John a great opportunity to see African Americans in films.

Dancer Bill Robinson didn't impress him. Mr. Robinson's dancing was great, but John noticed that his character never stood up for himself in a white world. Somewhere inside himself, John knew that all people are equal, and seeing a black person with a weak character on film didn't appeal to him.

John *was* fond of seeing black musician and bandleader Duke Ellington in a *Big Broadcast* movie filled with music and dancing in the early 1930s. The Duke was dressed in a classy white suit, which impressed John very much.[26] Little did he know that one day, he, John Birks Gillespie, would play with this famous musician in the Duke Ellington Orchestra. During John's tough childhood, the thought of a future playing with someone like the

Duke was more than he could have ever imagined.

Meanwhile, he got into fistfights every day after his father died. John gave credit to one boy who ended up being a regular opponent. "Daniel may have helped me a lot because all that hostility I vented on him made it easier for me to get along with my teachers."[27] John claimed that he wasn't a vicious person. Instead, he called himself "hotheaded."[28]

In spite of his woes in school, one of his teachers said, "He was a mess but he was a loving child. All the children loved him, and so did the teachers who had anything to do with him."[29] That teacher was

Mrs. Wilson, and it was through her that musical magic came into John's school life.

3. A Real Band!

By the time John was in fifth grade, the school principal had figured out a way to acquire money for instruments for a school band. He and Mrs. Wilson walked into class one day and asked who would like to join. John eagerly raised his hand.

The kids who wanted to learn to play were sent to a room where the beautiful horns and woodwinds were passed out. They went into the hands of the bigger kids first. By the time John's turn came, he was given the last horn left: a slide trombone.[30]

John started practicing right away. The only problem was that his arms were too short to push the trombone's slide out far enough to reach some of the notes. Even so, he was "knocked out just to have some kind of horn."[31] He practiced and practiced, and soon he could get a big noise out of it. In fact, John later said that "the whole neighborhood knew that I was learning how to play trombone."[32]

In a few short months, John's neighbor, Brother Harrington, had been given a new, nickel-plated trumpet for Christmas. Brother let John hang out at his house while he (Brother) practiced. John learned the B flat scale to "keep the trumpet warm"[33] for

Brother whenever he took a break. They played so much that Mrs. Harrington and Mrs. Gillespie both chased them out of their houses to a nearby field, where the boys were able to practice without disturbing anyone. In about nine months, John became as good at playing the trumpet as he was at playing the trombone. Even though his short, twelve-year-old arms kept him from being a great trombonist, he was considered one-of-a-kind in the school and in the town for being able to play both instruments.[34]

His teacher, Mrs. Wilson, said, "As long as he could hold a horn, he was all right."[35] She was able to teach John to play by ear, but she hadn't learned to read music well, and the only key she knew was B-flat. In John's mind, however, she gave him a great start, and he credited Mrs. Wilson all his life for teaching him to play music.[36]

Every year from then on, Mrs. Wilson organized a musical at the end of the school year. She put together a band for the show that included a piano player (herself); a trombone player; a snare drummer; a bass drummer; and John, who played cornet. "On sheer exuberance, we sounded good, and the audiences loved it," John wrote.[37]

John was feeling good about his ability to play, but he was still only working in one key. One day, a trumpet player named

Sonny Matthews, who had been playing up north in Philadelphia, came to Cheraw to visit his mother. Word got around about John and his trumpet-playing, so Sonny invited him over to see what he could do. They sat down at the piano, and Sonny started with a tune in the key of C. Relying only on his musical ear, John couldn't find a single note to play along. "I cried, because I was supposed to be the town's best trumpet player."[38] Feeling completely humiliated, John was determined to learn sight-reading and new scales other than B-flat. His friend and distant cousin, Norman Powe, was being given trombone lessons by another distant cousin, and Norman showed all that he learned to John. Within a few months, after lots of hard work, John had several keys under his belt. He wrote, "Even the guys in our little band were surprised at how much I knew."[39]

Because Mrs. Wilson could only play in the key of B-flat, the little band was eventually forced to find a new piano player who could play in all keys. They began searching for other places to play, and before long, they were paid to perform for a dance at the local white high school in Cheraw. Other gigs—at the local Elks Club and at places in other little towns not too far away—soon followed. Not only was he regarded as the best trumpet player in Cheraw, John also helped drummers in other bands with their rhythm challenges. He wrote, "I didn't know music, but I knew rhythm."[40]

4. Cruel Lessons Learned

Just before he started playing the trumpet, John was reminded—yet again—of the unwritten rule in Cheraw that there was a social difference between white and black people. This rule didn't show up in his everyday life right away. When he was a young child, kids from both groups played together naturally. However, as children grew older, parents and neighbors began to demonstrate the prejudices that are common in the United States by starting to keep black and white children apart.

John had a buddy named John Duvall, the son of a white family in town. The two of them had fun together all the time when they were seven or eight. But by the time John was eleven, his mother told him that he had to stop seeing his friend. Both boys were shocked and angry, but that didn't change the fact that they could no longer be friends.[41]

Even after John finished elementary school and left home to live at a preparatory school nearby called Laurinburg Institute, he continued to come home to play music professionally with his old friends on weekends. One of John's band members, a trombone player named Bill

McNeill, disappeared one day. Bill was African American. He was also a few years older than John and used to drink strong homegrown liquor, so at first, the band members weren't worried that he hadn't shown up for a few days. Then they heard that some white men had accused Bill of being a "Peeping Tom." The men caught him and bound him to the railroad tracks as a train was approaching. The murder caused anger, sadness, and a determination in John and his fellow band members to become so good at playing music that they could leave Cheraw behind forever.[42]

Of course, there were many instances of discrimination and attacks by white people in John's life. During one trip home from Laurinburg to see his family, he stopped at a gas station to get something to eat. A white man pulled out a pistol and asked him in an insulting way if he knew how to dance. Then the gunman began shooting at John's feet, which John moved quickly to avoid the bullets.[43] He escaped injury that time, but for many years afterward, he carried a knife with him for protection against these kinds of sudden attacks.

John continued to encounter prejudice during his whole life. During the years that he and his fellow musicians traveled in the United States from the 1930s through the

1970s—especially in the South—the white band members could always go in through the front door, but the black musicians had to enter through the back door. If their hotel had a pool, all guests had to register for tickets to swim, but black guests were never given tickets.[44] They had to learn to find restaurants where black people were welcome to eat and drink, and they had to stay away from places where doors were closed in their faces. Never mind that, as musicians, they had shared the gift of their talent with everyone who attended their performances. Black people were not permitted to eat with the people they entertained.

The many incidents in which black and white people were treated differently in the United States plagued John before and after the Civil Rights Act of 1964 became law. Throughout all the years of experiencing discrimination, however, he never felt that he was an inferior being, even though many white people tried to insist he should feel that way.[45] In his later years, when he had the power to do so, he made sure that his bands were made up of people from different cultures from all parts of the world, not only blacks and whites. His heart knew the truth of the equality of all people. But first, to continue his journey as a musician, he had to leave Cheraw.

5. Away from Home

The first step on the path to a new life was going away to school. There were no schools for black junior high or high school students in Cheraw, but there was one preparatory school, Laurinburg Technical Institute, that was twenty-eight miles away across the border in North Carolina. It just so happened that Laurinburg had lost both a trumpet and trombone player in their band and was looking for good replacements. John and Norman Powe, John's trombone-playing cousin, were recruited to fill the bill. John took along his toothbrush and toothpaste, a towel, and a change of underwear. He didn't have a trumpet of his own to bring along. However, the school was ready with everything he needed—food, a room, tuition, musical instruments, and the books for his classes. All they asked him to bring was his skill with the trumpet.

Seeing Laurinburg for the first time, John was impressed by the hospital on campus, the dorms, the classrooms, the basketball court and football field, and the acres of healthy crops growing around the school. He wrote, "I had no plans to become a farmer, but to a hungry boy like me, the thought of all that food growing around made the place very attractive."[46]

One of John's new roommates, Pope, was a good dresser from New York. He and John were about the same size, and Pope was happy to share white suits and "floppy stuff like they're wearing now" with John, who came to school with only the ragged shirt and pants he wore there.[47] Perhaps John remembered seeing the film he had watched in the movie theater of Duke Ellington in his white suit. Regardless, he always enjoyed wearing a nice set of clothes.

The food at the school was home-grown and good, but for this hungry young man, it was never enough. When John's eyes roamed around the dining hall, he saw one table with plates piled especially high with food. "Who are those guys over there?" he asked a friend. "They're the football players," she said. Right then and there, John decided to try out for the team.[48] Though he was short and small, he was energetic, spirited, and very fast. In fact, during his first game, he made the winning touchdown.[49]

Playing trumpet was the main reason John came to Laurinburg. He said he wasn't particularly interested in an education, though he was quite good at English.[50] Musically, he was ahead of the other students. He spent some time helping the players in the school band learn to read music, but mostly he spent his time practicing trumpet and piano. One day, the bandmaster at the school asked if he was going to keep playing football. "I'm not even thinking about that," John said. "I want to blow a horn." The man told John he could lose his front teeth playing on the team, which would make it very hard to play trumpet. From that moment—extra food notwithstanding— John gave up the game of football.[51]

Going to Laurinburg was a good step to take. John had progressed in his understanding of music. He had the time and quiet of living in the country to experiment with chords and harmonies. For the rest of his life, the knowledge he gained from having uninterrupted practice time on the piano kept him in the forefront of improvisation on the trumpet.

He also didn't neglect working on his ability to make people laugh. John always brought funny showmanship along with him in his music-making. One friend remembers him hanging from the limb of a tree—just to get a response from the dancers—while playing for a prom.[52]

John also had been taught to solve problems through hard work. In one instance, when bedbugs became a big problem in his dorm, he was required to make his own new mattress by hand rather than complain.[53] He also learned lessons from his work in agriculture at the school. He wrote, "We practiced scientific agriculture and grew or raised everything that we ate. In agriculture, I learned things about crop rotation, winter cover crops, and soil seepage. In the winter, you plant clover, and when spring comes, you plow that over and it rots in the soil and gives it nutrients. You plant on that richness. That's the key to raising good crops and a lesson about a rewarding life. Plant on your own personal richness your best gifts or talent."[54]

John's family in Cheraw had decided to move to Philadelphia, where more of their family lived. He had almost finished with his education at Laurinburg, and his mother visited him to say good-bye. John wanted to pack up right away and head north, too, but she asked him to finish high school first, and he stayed to please her. Because he missed his family so much and knew he could no longer travel the few miles to Cheraw to see them on weekends, he had trouble concentrating on schoolwork and failed his physics class. He had passed everything else, but he decided to leave school without a diploma rather than stay to take physics again.[55] He persuaded a friend to give him a ride to Philadelphia, and he knew his family would be overjoyed to see him even though he had left without graduating. As he journeyed further and further away from Cheraw, John thought about the train ride he had taken when he was eight years old. That journey had landed him in a place where people of all colors worked and played together more than they did in his hometown. He was ready to begin a future up north.

6. Getting Started with Jazz in Philadelphia

John was bringing some good skills and talents with him to "The City of Brotherly Love."[56] At Laurinburg, Norman Powe knew that John had been a better player than the bandmaster, Shorty Hall, even though Shorty could play "all the instruments."[57] Back in Cheraw, Norman had seen John learning from other bands ever since he was eleven. He knew that John also listened to the music from the churches in town. John had attended the Gillespie family's church, Wesley United Methodist, where a lone pianist had played and people had sung during "rousing services."[58] Then there had been the congregation of the Sanctified Church that he had attended on his own. Here, the music had been provided by pianos, drums, trumpets, saxophones, tambourines, and guitars.[59] The rhythms and the feelings they had aroused in him had made an impact on the young musician. John described the four preacher's sons playing four different rhythms at once, along with the sounds of stomping feet, clapping hands, and people jumping up and down on the resonant wooden floor of the church. The entire service had given John his "first experience with rhythm and spiritual transport."[60]

During their years together as children and band members, Norman heard

his friend's big talent with his own ears. He said, "I could tell that (John) had surpassed these people that were supposed to be so great in our eyesight . . . He was a genius."[61]

Even a genius trumpet player needs an instrument, however. During John's time away in school, his sister Mattie had married a man named Bill. John met Bill for the first time in Philly, and he wrote, "He [Bill] had a Cord automobile, gold teeth, and he owned the barbershop right down the street from us."[62] During that first week in Philly, Bill took John to a pawnshop and bought him a trumpet for $13. The horn didn't have a carrying case, so John carried the horn around in a paper bag. Other musicians laughed at the unusual sight of trumpet player with a bag for his horn.

John wasn't fazed, however, and he began playing for $8.00 a week in a rowdy bar. It was so rowdy there that, some years later, the place was renamed "Pearl Harbor."[63] Soon, John landed other jobs that paid a little better at other places, where people would listen to the music rather than talk over it, and he was able to join a musician's union to ensure that he always received a standard payment. The secretary for the union was a man with a band of his own, "one of the best in Philadelphia."[64]

Freddie Fairfax decided to try John out for this band. John was handed some sheet music for the tryout, but the notes were all squiggled in pencil, and in spite of his ability to read music well, he couldn't tell which of the squiggles were notes and which were rests. He didn't get the job, but he did get a nickname. A man in the band said, "That dizzy little cat's from down south," and John Birks Gillespie acquired a new name—"Dizzy."[65] Even though the word *dizzy* meant a little crazy and full of mischief, John decided to keep it. The name "Dizzy Gillespie" was unique, and people would remember it easily.

It wasn't long before Frankie Fairfax found out that Dizzy could read music after all, and the young trumpet player was asked to join the big band. He was only eighteen years old, and he was finally playing the kind of music he had always longed to play—soloing in the horn section of a big jazz band.

Even so, in two years' time, the musical life in Philadelphia became too small for the energetic Dizzy. He said good-bye to his mother, left his family's apartment, and struck out for The Big Apple—New York City.[66]

7. The Next Stop on the Journey

Dizzy's big brother, James Penfield (J. P.), let him move in to his tiny apartment in New York. Dizzy would play all night while J. P. slept. In the morning, Dizzy would come home from playing and jamming, and J. P. would go off to work and let Dizzy use the bed. J. P. would always leave 35 cents for Dizzy's meal of the day, since the young trumpeter was mostly playing without being paid.[67] It was a hard time but exciting as well. Dizzy was listening to and jamming with some of the best jazz artists around, even if he didn't have much to eat. Eventually, enough people heard him play that he was asked to audition for the Teddy Hill Band, which was traveling to Paris.

By the time he was age 20, Dizzy had arranged a tune for a big band and had played as a soloist with the Teddy Hill Band on his first recording. It was a good start. In the years ahead, Dizzy would play on hundreds of recordings and travel to perform as many as three hundred gigs a year.[68]

However, this success still lay in the future. Back in New York, Dizzy fell on especially hard financial times. He wanted to join a musician's union in New York, but he was required to wait three months after his European tour with Teddy Hill before he could sign up and receive union protections, such as a good standard pay and regular hours playing with a band. On top of that, his brother had moved out of their apartment, and Dizzy barely had enough to eat every day. In fact, he wouldn't have eaten at all without the help of a new friend.

Dizzy met dancer Lorraine Willis one night when she performed in Washington, D.C. She was a strong, quiet person who would go home after shows, read the Bible, and knit instead of hanging out with the musicians, as most of the other dancers did. She helped support her mother by sending her about half of her weekly income, and she took her religion and her service to her family seriously. Dizzy noticed Lorraine for her beauty and for her habit of keeping to herself. He was curious about her and wanted to get to know her better, so he worked hard at setting up a date just to go out to get a Coca-Cola with the appealing young woman.

When Lorraine finally said yes, she found out that Dizzy was penniless. He'd been asking people regularly for money just for a bite to eat: a bowl of soup once a day for fifteen cents. Lorraine consulted with her mother who, when she heard Dizzy's story, encouraged Lorraine to use the $10—which Lorraine usually set aside for her mother—to feed Dizzy. He was amazed that Lorraine's mother would be so supportive of him, and he was grateful.[69] Lorraine remained his friend, and they were married during the next big musical

phase in Dizzy's career—playing with the renowned Cab Calloway. For the rest of his life, Lorraine remained a calm, serious, settling influence for him.

Dizzy was funny and full of energy. He was also an excellent musician, so his humor didn't stop him from being a great asset to a new big band. It turned out that Lorraine knew the valet of bandleader Cab Calloway, and this valet arranged for Dizzy to sit in and play one night with Mr. Calloway's band. Because of Dizzy's playing during that quick audition, Cab gave him a position in the band, and a new period of Dizzy's life began.[70] He was playing regularly with one band, earning good money, traveling in style when the band was on the road, and jamming with musicians he met. Swing music was the popular style at the time. It was dance music, and dancers called Lindy Hoppers would literally wear away the floors of clubs because their dancing was so enthusiastic.[71]

Dizzy nailed the trumpet sounds Cab Calloway was asking for, and he also did a lot of funny stuff behind Cab's back on stage. During a Cab solo, Dizzy would sometimes mime throwing a football across the stage to another player, who pretended to catch it. Sometimes, when Cab was singing a tender ballad, Dizzy would wave to an imaginary friend in the audience. When people started to laugh, Cab would turn around to see what was going on with his band, and Dizzy would be staring at the ceiling, as innocent as could be. This made the audiences laugh even harder, of course.

One night, after Dizzy had been playing with Cab Calloway for about two years, someone threw big spitballs on the stage under the spotlights during part of the show. Cab was certain it was Dizzy, but this time, Dizzy wasn't the culprit. After the music ended, Cab kept accusing Dizzy, who stood up for himself. They were so angry with each other that Cab grabbed Dizzy around the collar. Seething with rage, Dizzy pulled out his knife and cut Mr. Calloway on the backside.[72]

Dizzy was immediately fired, and he and Cab left each other with understandably bad feelings on both sides. Those feelings didn't last, however. When Mr. Calloway was interviewed for Dizzy's memoirs thirty-eight years later, he had this to say: "A lotta people don't understand Dizzy. Dizzy is a fine musician—and a very intelligent, fine-thinking person. A person who knows what's happening in life . . . He really filled the bill . . . and added as much, or more, to my band than anybody I know."[73]

During these months and years with Cab Calloway, Dizzy was still jamming after shows with musicians who weren't in the band with him. He was always eager to improvise, especially with players he hadn't met before. Sometimes they would gather on the roof of the Cotton Club in Harlem in the middle of the night.[74] Other times they would congregate in Dizzy's apartment. After they had played all night, Lorraine would feed everyone a big breakfast, and the men would play softly on their instruments so as not to bother the neighbors.[75] On Monday nights—the musicians' night off in the clubs—the players would meet up to jam at a club named "Minton's Playhouse."[76] The dimly-lit room would be filled with smoke, quiet laughter, talk, and the smells of delicious food while the musicians worked out music that hadn't been heard before.[77]

In all of these places, four musicians especially were helping Dizzy break new ground in the world of jazz: drummer

Kenny Clarke; pianist Thelonious Monk; guitarist Charlie Christian; and above all, alto saxophone player Charlie Parker, whom Dizzy called "the other half of my heartbeat."[78] These musicians were all friends, but Dizzy and Charlie Parker were especially close. The five of them began creating music to listen to rather than to dance to. It would take some time for jazz audiences to come to love it, but eventually they did. This new and complex music had a name: bebop.

8. Bebop!

The birth of bebop did not occur overnight. While playing with bands in his teens and twenties, Dizzy experimented with mixing different rhythms together at the same time. His improvisations got faster and faster while he experimented with new ways of playing chords with a band as well as getting from one note to another in a melody. As his skills increased, he had the added experience of becoming the music director of the Billy Eckstine Orchestra in 1943, where he had input into choosing the players in the band as well as the music they played.[79] Billy said of Dizzy's new style, "Dizzy was never one who went on just what God gave him. He always embellished it with studying and understanding . . . The man's a master of his instrument."[80]

Over time, Dizzy met and worked with his bebop collaborators, and they added to each other's knowledge and style.[81] Through recordings, the sharing of new songs, and public and private jam sessions, bebop was becoming more and more popular. Finally, in the mid-1940s, when Dizzy formed and led his own groups—first a quartet, then the Dizzy

Gillespie Orchestra—so many people were eager to hear the new music that a band playing bebop could make enough money to survive and prosper.

Dizzy's compositions, such as "A Night in Tunisia" and "Salt Peanuts," helped showcase bebop. In 1943, Dizzy had the pleasure of playing in the band of his childhood movie hero, Duke Ellington.[82] He described this new musical experience this way: "To play with Duke you have to forget everything you know . . . You have to conform to his approach and be receptive."[83] The music didn't include the developing jazz style of the beboppers, but Dizzy saw a master bandleader at work—a man who knew how to get the best out of his players.

Unfortunately, this was one group where the musicians already in the band would not help a new player become comfortable with Mr. Ellington's music. Older players resented younger ones with new ideas and were afraid of being displaced. Jazz pianist Mary Lou Williams describes what was happening this way: "Dizzy did not receive a warm, open reception when he was coming up. He came up the hard way . . . He's so nice to everyone else until it added to his power as far as being the greatest in the world . . . And I've seen him go all the way out for someone in order to make them a success."[84]

Working in Duke Ellington's band was one of several experiences that helped Dizzy want to treat new band members he worked with—especially young kids—differently. Dizzy always made himself available to help these young, talented players get a start in the jazz world.[85] He didn't talk down to them; he just showed them what he knew. When he was on the road in the years when he had his own bands, he often took the time to run workshops and clinics for high school and college students. During the 1970s, he even had a special "hotline" in his house. He gave the number out to younger players so that they could get in touch with him to ask their questions about music.[86]

Eventually, Dizzy sported a new look to accompany his new music. In the 1940s, he began to wear a beret. He said that he was always losing hats and that a beret was easy to slip off and put inside a pocket. A beret could also double as a mute for Dizzy's trumpet if need be. Dizzy also discovered that shaving his beard would create an itchy lower lip and chin, and since playing the trumpet irritated his skin when this happened, he began wearing a goatee. He also wore horn-rimmed glasses because they had stronger frames that lasted longer than the gold-rimmed glasses that were in style at the time. Soon, fans of bebop showed up at performances imitating his appearance.[87] Dizzy's look was not the only thing that changed at this point in his career. In 1953, someone fell on his trumpet, and the impact bent the bell upward. At first, Dizzy thought the trumpet sounded strange, but he soon learned to appreciate the differences he heard. From then on, his trumpets were altered to look and sound the same.[88] As the years wore on, Dizzy's cheeks bulged out more and more whenever he played. As a natural result of playing the trumpet in

his own style, he developed his trademark puffy chipmunk cheeks.[89] Anyone who saw the bent trumpet and puffy cheeks immediately knew they were looking at Dizzy Gillespie.

As these style changes came about, bebop was not welcomed with open arms by fans of the jazz that was popular in the

late 1930s and 40s. From blues to Dixie-
land to swing, jazz had evolved as any art
form does. Often, change in music, dance,
or painting is considered odd, uninterest-
ing, or even unacceptable when it first
appears. For instance, painters who are now
famous—such as impressionists Monet
and Renoir—were considered unac-
complished and primitive when they first
started showing their work. Over time,
people grew to see beauty in their new style
of painting, and impressionist paintings
can now be sold for millions of dollars.[90]

The same process occurred with bebop. It took time for jazz fans to learn to
appreciate the new sound. Those who dis-

liked bebop were called "Moldy Figs" by the beboppers, and bebop was criticized by these Moldy Figs as a bad influence on young people and a symbol of rebellion.[91] However, bebop has outlasted its critics. One writer for "U Discover Music" in 2019 claims that bebop continues to be "the most important development in jazz," and that musicians after the bebop era are still inspired by what they hear of Dizzy's work.[92] Today, Dizzy and his fellow beboppers are considered to be as accomplished in music as the Impressionists are in visual art.[93]

9. Playing Around the Globe

During the years after Dizzy stopped playing with Cab Calloway, he began to meet more musicians from Central and South American countries, such as Cuba and Brazil. The rhythms of these players and their music inspired him for the rest of his life. For Dizzy, rhythm was the foundation of the new music he was bringing into being.[94] He said, "I think up a rhythm first and then I put notes to it to correspond with the chord. You can play very, very beautiful notes and if it doesn't have any rhythmic form, it doesn't amount to anything."[95]

Dizzy often told people how African Americans who were brought to the United States and enslaved were forced to give up their drums. During that time, slave masters had been afraid that the Africans could communicate over long distances through drumbeats, and that they would be planning escapes or ways to overthrow their owners, who felt no qualms about buying and selling human beings.[96] Now, however, Dizzy was taking back the drum and celebrating its power in music. Latin and Afro-Cuban rhythms were at the heart of his tunes such as "Manteca" (translated as "Give Me Some Skin"), "Cubana Be" and "Cubana Bop."

Dizzy was a continual whirlwind of rehearsing and performing energy. From the time he moved to Philadelphia in 1935, he dedicated fifty-seven years to playing the trumpet as often as he could. Even during the last year of his life, he traveled to gigs around the globe and logged nearly 300,000 miles of traveling in 1992 alone.[97] He gave performances not only as a soloist but also as a bandleader with groups large and small, and in 1956, he also was the first jazz musician to travel on cultural missions for the U.S. Department of State. He insisted on playing for everyday people—street vendors, snake charmers, and village children—as well as the usual audiences of ambassadors, kings, queens, and presidents that had been set up for him, and he always strove to establish goodwill for the United States with *all* the people he met, wherever he went. In

countries such as Lebanon, Syria, Iran, Egypt, India, Turkey, Greece, Yugoslavia, and Pakistan, Dizzy always insisted on getting out of the big cities—where formal concerts were planned—and traveling out into small towns and rural areas.[98]

Showman Dizzy made people laugh, whether intentionally or not. For one show in Greece, Dizzy took a step down off the main stage and—disappeared! He had fallen into an orchestra pit covered with something thin, such as cloth. The musicians on stage were worried he'd either killed himself or had broken an arm or a leg. They kept playing background music, though, hoping Dizzy would reappear. Suddenly, up he came, holding his trumpet high in the air and walking out of the hole into which he'd fallen. That brought a big laugh from everyone, and the show went on.[99]

What was his effect on the people in the countries where he was sent as a musical ambassador? Condoleezza Rice, who served as U.S. Secretary of State nearly twenty years after Dizzy's tour for the State Department, had this to say about him:

Back then [in 1956], America's civil rights movement was still in its infancy and we still had a long way to go to live up to the democratic ideals of our country's founding. But it was in American culture, in the story of people like Dizzy Gillespie that one could see the future promise of our country. A young man of modest means, the youngest of nine [living] children, whose creative genius transcended boundaries of race, and class, and culture. Even at a time when liberty was denied here in America—a time that I remember well as a girl growing up in the segregated city of Birmingham, Alabama—the music of Dizzy Gillespie spoke the language of freedom; the freedom to think, to innovate, and to speak in one's own voice. This liberating power of jazz resonated here at home and it had great appeal to millions of people around the world, many of whom still longed for their own liberty. For these audiences, in Latin America, in Europe, and in the Middle East, Dizzy Gillespie's world tour left an indelible impression of the vibrancy of American culture, the diversity of American society, and most of all, the power of hope that freedom holds for all people.[100]

About three years after his 1956 tour, Dizzy discovered something new about his ancestry. On one visit back to his hometown, he was told that his great grandmother was the daughter of a Yoruba chief in the country of Nigeria on the continent of Africa.[101] In 1989, Dizzy toured African countries for a month. At a stop in Nigeria, he was honored by being made a tribal chief—a *Baashere of Iperu*—in a formal ceremony. An interviewer described what happened: "He felt a close kinship with these people. He said they all looked like his relatives. He was very serious during the ceremony, where he wore this gorgeous, forty-pound traditional robe in green, beige, and white. The ritual involved sacred drumming and chanting, and he took off his shoes and danced with the others in the red dirt. The whole observance touched something deep inside him. Truly."[102]

10. Seeing the World—and Jazz— through New Eyes

Before these ancestral discoveries, Dizzy's fame—the result of collaborating with a few fellow musicians to create bebop—increased. Millions of people became familiar with the name *Dizzy Gillespie.* He played with the most well-known jazz musicians of his day and was delighted to be able to make a living doing what he loved most.

Music was not the only thing he thought about, even as his fame grew. It

was impossible to ignore the racism that showed up every day in his life, and he wanted to do something to change that for himself and for all African Americans. One of his publicists had an idea. In the 1960s, the man had buttons made that read "Dizzy Gillespie for President" as an advertising gimmick. It brought Dizzy a lot of attention, but it was more than advertising to Dizzy. He seriously considered running for President of the United States in 1964.[103] His hope was that a black man running could bring up issues of race in the United States that needed to be resolved. Of course, the country needed more than a black president to solve its racial problems. By the time Martin Luther King, Jr. was assassinated in 1968, Dizzy despaired over the future of African Americans. He drank more and more to erase the pain he felt, but he also knew that he would have to stop drinking if he cared about changing the world.[104]

While playing a gig in Milwaukee, Wisconsin, Dizzy met Beth McKintey.

She was a big jazz fan, and she called him and asked if she could talk with him about making music with Charlie Parker. He answered, "No, madam, I don't want no strange woman coming over to my hotel."[105] She told him that she and her husband would be in the club that night, and they all talked together about his childhood and family. Dizzy began to trust the McKinteys.

Beth sent him pamphlets about the Bahá'í Faith. From their talks, she knew that Dizzy believed in the equality of all people, which is at the heart of this world religion. He was very receptive to what he was reading and hearing, and before long, he had read all of the pamphlets Beth had sent him, plus a book titled *Thief in the Night*. This book explored biblical prophecies relating to the time when the spirit of Christ would return to Earth as He had promised. "It was like a detective story tracing what is supposed to happen when a new message comes from God to mankind," Dizzy wrote in his memoirs.[106]

Dizzy was now fifty-one years old. Not long after meeting Beth, he made a trip to Los Angeles in 1968 and met William Sears, the author of *Thief in the Night*. Dizzy had decided to join the Bahá'í Faith and did so that very day. He wrote, "I had my declaration card already in a sealed envelope, because when I read the book, I said, 'Boy, I really wanna be like this.' I think this is what God wants. So I gave my declaration to make it official. That's how I became a Bahá'í. Becoming a Bahá'í changed my life in every way and gave me a new concept of the relationship between God and man—man and his family. I became more spiritually aware, and when you're spiritually aware, that will be reflected in what you do."[107] Slowly, Dizzy stopped drinking alcohol or carrying a weapon for protection. He started to pray and read more. He wrote, "The (Bahá'í) writings gave me new insight on what the plan is—God's plan—for this time, the truth of the oneness of God, the truth of the oneness of the prophets, the truth of the oneness of mankind. That's it; that's what I learned."[108]

William Sears, author of *Thief in the Night*

For Dizzy, another basic idea of the Bahá'í teachings made a lot of sense—not only do all religions come from the same God, but they also build on one another. Though spiritual rules for each religion may change—such as which day is the Sabbath, what a person shouldn't eat or drink, and what prayers are important— the basic truths, such as the Golden Rule to "do unto others as you would have them do unto you," remain consistent through- out the world's religions.[109]

Dizzy was able to accept the idea that religion evolved partly because he knew from his experience as a musician that music also evolved. He knew, for instance, that well-loved musicians had helped create music from the early traditional use of drums and song all the way to the use of sophisticated instruments, rhythms, and harmonies associated with modern jazz. He also knew that the talents of trumpet players such as Louis Armstrong and Roy Eldridge had paved the way for new innovations in performing and a growing understanding of the relationship between the trumpet and jazz. After becoming a Bahá'í, Dizzy often spoke about the evolution of music in interviews, and he became a passionate advocate for all the musicians who had come before him and who had helped make him the musician he was. He knew that his own work would eventually pave the way for new trumpeters, such as Miles Davis and Wynton Marsalis. History, music, and religion unfolded progressively! He liked this idea a lot.

11. Dizzying Heights

Dizzy's musical journey took him into television and film, as well as live and recorded performances. He first appeared in a film titled *Case of the Blues* in 1942—the same year he established his first jazz quartet.[110] He eventually was invited to perform on the *Tonight Show* with Johnny Carson, the *Ed Sullivan Show*, the *Cosby Show*, *The Muppet Show*, and the *Today Show*, along with many others. He also wrote and performed music for film scores of both live action and animated movies.

The last film he worked on, titled *The Winter in Lisbon,* was released in 1992.[111] Dizzy composed the score and also played a leading role in which he delivered a speech denouncing racism.

Dizzy's musical genius and frenetic career pace brought him both national and international recognition. In 1944, Dizzy won his first national honor, the *Esquire* magazine New Star Award.[112] From then on, he earned over ninety other awards, including two Grammys—prestigious awards given by the Recording Academy for achievements in the music industry—seventeen honorary degrees from places as diverse as Rutgers University; the

Chicago Conservatory of Music; and his preparatory school, the Laurinburg Technical Institute. He also received the rank of Commander in the prestigious French Order of Arts and Letters, as well as the highest award the United States gives to artists for their lifetime contribution to the performing arts—the Kennedy Center Honors.

In his autobiography, Dizzy singles out one award and gives honor to Paul Robeson, an African-American concert artist and actor of stage and film who lived in the twentieth century. In addition to his artistic contributions, Mr. Robeson stood up for the rights of black people in the United

States. Dizzy wrote, "Of all these honors, the one that gave me the greatest sense of pride was the Paul Robeson Award (from Rutgers University Institute of Jazz Studies), because Paul Robeson was really my hero . . . On account of Paul Robeson, the struggle (for civil rights) gained momentum which led into Martin Luther King, Malcolm X, and whoever else. Paul was an incorruptible soul. He was the biggest."[113] Dizzy valued service to others very highly, both in Mr. Robeson's example and in his own life. "The highest role is the role of service to humanity," he wrote, "and if I can make that, then I'll be happy."[114]

In February of 1992, Dizzy began to show signs of a major illness, but he was reluctant to find out what was wrong. His decades-long drive to perform was too strong for him to take time to recover from being sick. When his friends could finally get him to a hospital, he was diagnosed with pancreatic cancer. Though most of the cancer was removed through surgery, the doctors could not get it all, so he was given other treatments that extended his life for a few more months. He appeared for a tribute concert given for him that August at the Hollywood Bowl. Though he couldn't play, he assured the audience that he would return to the trumpet soon. However, by November, he made his last public appearance.[115] On January 6, 1993, Dizzy Gillespie died in his sleep while a collection of his music, *Dizzy's Diamonds*, played softly in the background.[116]

Dizzy's journey had started with a train ride to Philadelphia at age eight and had taken him to a career spreading the gospel of bebop. His musical genius and humor brought him fame and the love of many musicians and fans. This fame didn't make him pull away from others as it grew, and his friend Marion Frazier wrote, "John's the only celebrity I know who has never changed . . . I don't think he realizes that he is a celebrity and the greatness that he carries. That's what I admire about him most . . ."[117]

Six days after his death, a memorial service was held in Saint John's Cathedral—a spectacular building longer than a football field—in New York City. Six thousand people came to honor him, and music rang throughout the huge space. In the tradition of jazz funerals in New Orleans, which had their origins in West Africa, Wynton Marsalis and his musicians started with a slow-moving, sad dirge. By the end of the three-hour celebration of his life, twenty-five musicians had touched the hearts of the crowd with a joyful musical tribute to Dizzy.[118] John Birks Gillespie, trumpet virtuoso and improviser who was called "King of the Trumpet" by his fellow bebop musicians, and "A Jazz Ambassador for the Ages" for his service to the U.S. State Department, was celebrated with some of the best, most moving music available—his own.[119]

Timeline

Important Events in the Life of
John Birks "Dizzy" Gillespie

1917   Born on October 21, 1917 in Cheraw, South Carolina.

1921   Shows his first interest in music by picking out a tune on the piano and practicing rhythm patterns on his father's drums.

1926   Visits Philadelphia and New York.

1927   Papa Gillespie dies from asthma at home.

1929   A school band provides Dizzy with his first horn: a trombone.

1930   Plays cornet in a school musical performance.

1933   Graduates from Robert Smalls public school and enters Laurinburg Institute.

1935   Follows his family to Philadelphia, joins a musician's union there, starts playing with the Freddie Fairfax Band, and writes his first big band arrangement. He receives the name "Dizzy" from a fellow musician.

1937	Moves to New York City; travels to Europe with the Teddy Hill Orchestra; meets his future wife, Lorraine Willis; and works on a revolutionary style of improvising.
1939	Joins Cab Calloway Orchestra.
1940	Marries Lorraine in Boston, Massachusetts, meets beloved bebop collaborator Charlie Parker, and records his first original songs in Chicago.
1942	Establishes and leads his own quartet.
1943	First records music with Charlie Parker and plays briefly with the Duke Ellington Orchestra. Is appointed musical director for the Billy Eckstine Orchestra.
1944	Wins first national honor: *Esquire* New Star Award.
1945–46	Organizes first and second Dizzy Gillespie Orchestras and appears on film for the first time.
1947	Is featured at Carnegie Hall Concert for the first time.
1950	Disbands the Dizzy Gillespie Orchestra, organizes Dizzy Gillespie Sextet/Quintet, and tours Europe.
1951	Establishes a record company, Dee Gee Records, which lasts for two years.

1953	Trumpet bell gets bent upward in a fortunate accident, and Dizzy keeps his trumpets bent from then on.
1956	Becomes first jazz musician to undertake cultural missions in other countries for the U.S. State Department.
1959	Mother, Lottie, dies at age seventy-four. Dizzy performs in the first integrated public school in his hometown of Cheraw, South Carolina, and he discovers that his grandmother was the daughter of a Yoruba chief.
1964	Seriously considers campaigning to become President of the United States.
1968	Becomes a member of the Bahá'í Faith while on a trip to Los Angeles, California.
1972	Receives Paul Robeson Award from Rutgers University Institute of Jazz Studies.
1976	Honored by the South Carolina Arts Commission.
1977–78	Performs twice at the White House for President Carter.
1979	His autobiography, *To Be, or not . . . to Bop*, is published.

1989	Receives a Lifetime Achievement Grammy from the Recording Academy that recognizes excellence in the music industry; also receives a National Medal of the Arts from President George Bush.
1990	Receives the Kennedy Center Honors from President George Bush, who calls him a "magician of the musical form."
1993	Dies in his sleep while a recording of his music plays softly.

Notes

1. Gillespie, *To Be, or not . . . to Bop*, pp. 11–12.
2. Ibid., pp. 4–5; Maggin, *Dizzy: The Life and Times of John Birks Gillespie*, p. 22.
3. Spruill, "Dizzy Gillespie in Cheraw." http://www.cheraw.com/about_cheraw.php?About-Cheraw-Town-History-Dizzy-Gillespie-in-Cheraw-10.
4. Maggin, *Dizzy: The Life and Times of John Birks Gillespie*, pp. 16–17.
5. Gillespie, *To Be, or not . . . to Bop*, p. 12.
6. Maggin, *Dizzy: The Life and Times of John Birks Gillespie*, p. 21.
7. Gillespie, *To Be, or not . . . to Bop*, p. 2.
8. Maggin, *Dizzy: The Life and Times of John Birks Gillespie*, p. 24.
9. Ibid., p. 21. [Author's note: James and Lottie were married in 1899 when Lottie was fourteen. Their first child was born in 1900.]
10. Gillespie, *To Be, or not . . . to Bop*, p. 6.
11. Ibid.
12. Ibid., p. 2.
13. Ibid., p. 1.

14. Shipton, *Groovin' High: The Life of Dizzy Gillespie*, p. 7; Gillespie, *To Be, or not . . . to Bop*, p. 6.

15. Gillespie, *To Be, or not . . . to Bop*, p. 7.

16. Ibid., p. 8.

17. Ibid., p. 9.

18. Ibid.

19. Gillespie, *To Be, or not . . . to Bop*, p. 13. [Author's note: Though his book and other sources say that John was ten years old when his father died, his father's death occurred in June of 1927, four months before his tenth birthday.]

20. Ibid., p. 14.

21. Maggin, *Dizzy: The Life and Times of John Birks Gillespie*, p. 14.

22. Ibid., p. 26; Gillespie, *To Be, or not . . . to Bop*, p. 16.

23. Gillespie, *To Be, or not . . . to Bop*, p. 14.

24. Shipton, *Groovin' High: The Life of Dizzy Gillespie*, pp. 8–9.

25. Maggin, *Dizzy: The Life and Times of John Birks Gillespie*, p. 26.

26. Gillespie, *To Be, or not . . . to Bop*, p. 16.

27. Ibid., p. 10.

28. Ibid., p. 19.

29. Maggin, *Dizzy: The Life and Times of John Birks Gillespie*, p. 30.

30. Ibid., pp. 28–29.

31. Gillespie, *To Be, or not . . . to Bop,* p. 21.

32. Ibid., p. 21.

33. Ibid.

34. Ibid., p. 22.

35. Ibid., p. 22.

36. Ibid., p. 274.

37. Ibid., p. 24.

38. Ibid., p. 28.

39. Ibid.

40. Ibid., p. 27.

41. Ibid., p. 17.

42. Ibid., p. 30.

43. Ibid., pp. 43–44.

44. Ibid., p. 445.

45. Ibid., p. 17.

46. Ibid., p. 35.

47. Ibid.

48. Ibid., p. 36.

49. Ibid., p. 37.

50. Ibid., p. 35.

51. Ibid., p. 39.

52. Maggin, *Dizzy: The Life and Times of John Birks Gillespie,* p. 40.

53. Gillespie, *To Be, or not . . . to Bop,* p. 38.

54. Ibid.

55. Ibid., p. 46.

56. Gollust, "Words and Their Stories: Philadelphia and Boston." https://learningenglish.voanews.com/a/nicknames-for-philadelphia-and-boston-89834907/112420.html.

57. Gillespie, *To Be, or not . . . to Bop*, p. 45.

58. Maggin, *Dizzy: The Life and Times of John Birks Gillespie*, p. 11.

59. Ibid.

60. Gillespie, *To Be, or not . . . to Bop*, p. 31.

61. Ibid., p. 45.

62. Ibid., p. 48.

63. Ibid.

64. Gillespie, *To Be, or not . . . to Bop*, p. 49.

65. Ibid. [Author's note: There are several stories from different sources about how Dizzy acquired his nickname, but in his memoir, it was with Freddie Fairfax's band that it was first mentioned and then stuck.]

66. Ibid., p. 60.

67. Ibid., pp. 62–63.

68. Discogs, https://www.discogs.com/artist/64694-Dizzy-Gillespie; Bowers, "Farewell, Diz," *The American Bahá'í*, February 17, 1993, p. 9.

69. Gillespie, *To Be, or not . . . to Bop*, pp. 81–83.

70. Ibid., p. 96.

71. Maggin, *Dizzy: The Life and Times of John Birks Gillespie*, p. 56.

72. Gillespie, *To Be, or not . . . to Bop*, pp. 130–32; Maggin, *Dizzy: The Life and Times of John Birks Gillespie*, p. 125.

73. Gillespie, *To Be, or not . . . to Bop*, p. 111.

74. Ibid., p. 114.

75. Maggin, *Dizzy: The Life and Times of John Birks Gillespie*, p. 119.

76. Gillespie, *To Be, or not . . . to Bop*, p. 139.

77. Maggin, *Dizzy: The Life and Times of John Birks Gillespie*, p. 118.

78. Giddens, "It's Dizzy Again." https://www.nytimes.com/1978/06/25/archives/its-dizzy-again-much-to-his-surprise-dizzy-gillespiewho-has-been.html.

79. Gillespie, *To Be, or not . . . to Bop*, pp. 182–83.

80. Ibid., p. 174.

81. Maggin, *Dizzy: The Life and Times of John Birks Gillespie*, pp. 90–91.

82. Vail, *Dizzy Gillespie: The Bebop Years 1937–1952*, p. 23.

83. Gillespie, *To Be, or not . . . to Bop*, p. 184.

84. Ibid., p. 150.

85. Bowers, "Farewell, Diz," *The American Bahá'í*, February 7, 1993, p. 9.

86. Maggin, *Dizzy: The Life and Times of John Birks Gillespie*, pp. 324–25.

87. Gillespie, *To Be, or not . . . to Bop*, pp. 279–80.

88. Maggin, *Dizzy: The Life and Times of John Birks Gillespie*, pp. 253–54.

89. Gillespie, *To Be, or not . . . to Bop*, pp. 315–16.

90. For more information, please see https://news.psu.edu/story/324175/2014/08/28/research/probing-question-why-impressionist-art-so-popular and https://www.dw.com/en/claude-monet-painting-sells-for-record-1107m-at-auction/a-48740167.

91. Gillespie, *To Be, or not . . . to Bop*, pp. 294–95, 302.

92. See https://www.udiscovermusic.com/stories/what-is-bebop-jazz/.

93. Maggin, *Dizzy: The Life and Times of John Birks Gillespie*, p. 196.

94. Gillespie, *To Be, or not . . . to Bop*, pp. 491–92.

95. Maggin, *Dizzy: The Life and Times of John Birks Gillespie*, p. 2.

96. Gillespie, *To Be, or not . . . to Bop*, pp. 483–84.

97. Landsberg, "Of Jazz Greats, It's Now Mainly Dizzy," *St. Louis Post-Dispatch*, March 29, 1992, p. 3C.

98. Gillespie, *To Be, or not . . . to Bop*, p. 418.

99. Ibid., p. 426.

100. Costagneto, "Ambassador Dizzy: Jazz Diplomacy in the Cold War Era." http://americanaejournal.hu/vol10jazz/castagneto.

101. Gillespie, *To Be, or not . . . to Bop*, p. 442.

102. Maggin, *Dizzy: The Life and Times of John Birks Gillespie,* pp. 367–68.

103. Gillespie, *To Be, or not . . . to Bop,* pp. 452–53.

104. Ibid., pp. 472–73.

105. Ibid., p. 473.

106. Ibid.

107. Ibid., p. 474.

108. Ibid.

109. Matthew 7:12.

110. Gillespie, *To Be, or not . . . to Bop,* pp. 525, xii.

111. Rotten Tomatoes, https://www.rottentomatoes.com/m/winter_in_lisbon.

112. Gillespie, *To Be, or not . . . to Bop,* p. xii.

113. Ibid., p. 498.

114. Gillespie, *To Be, or not . . . to Bop,* p. 502.

115. Maggin, *Dizzy: The Life and Times of John Birks Gillespie,* pp. 384–87.

116. Bowers, "Farewell, Diz," *The American Bahá'í,* p. 9.

117. Gillespie, *To Be, or not . . . to Bop,* p. 381.

118. Maggin, *Dizzy: The Life and Times of John Birks Gillespie,* p. 391.

119. Gillespie, *To Be, or not . . . to Bop,* p. 353; Orr, "Dizzy Gillespie: A Jazz Ambassador for the Ages." https://www.montereyjazzfestival.org/.

Performances of Dizzy Gillespie Available Online

"Groovy Man" shows Dizzy in 1947 leading his big band. His sense of humor shines through in the lyrics: "He thought he was the cream of the crop, but he beeped when he should have bopped." https://www.youtube.com/watch?v=dtG-5m7P56vk.

"Hot House" shows Dizzy in 1951 with Charlie Parker, whom Dizzy called "the other half of my heartbeat." https://www.youtube.com/watch?v=tJYO6_t4d08.

"Umbrella Man" shows two great trumpet players, Dizzy and Louis Armstrong, in 1959 on the *Jackie Gleason TV Show.* https://www.youtube.com/watch?v=ZO1uMjz3n3w.

"Dizzy Gillespie Quintet" shows Dizzy playing in 1966 on a British TV show called Jazz 625. This episode of the program showcases Dizzy's and James Moody's music along

with Dizzy's characteristic chatter between songs. https://
www.youtube.com/watch?v=2uLpjp7xkyI.

"Salt Peanuts" shows one performance in the 1970s in which
Dizzy teaches the audience to sing along. https://www.you-
tube.com/watch?v=TvIXzeDLpMw.

Bibliography

Bowers, Jack. "Farewell, Diz." *The American Bahá'í* 24, no. 2 (February 7, 1993).

Costagneto, Pierangelo. "Ambassador Dizzy: Jazz Diplomacy in the Cold War Era." *Americana: E-Journal of American Studies in Hungary.* http://americanaejournal.hu/vol10jazz/castagneto.

Discogs. "Dizzy Gillespie." https://www.discogs.com/artist/64694-Dizzy-Gillespie.

Giddins, Gary. "It's Dizzy Again." *The New York Times* (June 25, 1978). https://www.nytimes.com/1978/06/25/archives/its-dizzy-again-much-to-his-surprise-dizzy-gillespiewho-has-been.html.

Gillespie, Dizzy, with Al Frazer. *To Be or not to Bop: Memoirs—Dizzy Gillespie.* Garden City, New York: Doubleday and Company, Inc., 1979.

Gollust, Shelley. "Words and Their Stories: Nicknames for Philadelphia and Boston." April 3, 2010. https://learningenglish.voanews.com/a/nicknames-for-philadelphia-and-boston-89834907/112420.html.

Grogan, David. "The Chief of Entertainment." *The American Scholar*. December 4, 2017. https://theamericanscholar.org/dizzy/#.XPiKAS2ZP6C.

Landsberg, Mitchell. "Of Jazz Greats, It's Now Mainly Dizzy." *St. Louis Post-Dispatch* (March 29, 1992).

Maggin, Donald L. *Dizzy: The Life and Times of John Birks Gillespie*. New York: Harper, 2005.

Orr, Timothy. "Dizzy Gillespie: A Jazz Ambassador for the Ages." *MJF Blog*. February 16, 2017. https://www.montereyjazzfestival.org/.

Rotten Tomatoes. "Winter in Lisbon." March 9, 1992. https://www.rottentomatoes.com/m/winter_in_lisbon.

Shipton, Alyn. *Groovin' High: The Life of Dizzy Gillespie*. Oxford: Oxford University Press, 1999.

Spruill, Sarah. "Dizzy Gillespie in Cheraw." 2006. http://www.cheraw.com/about_cheraw.php?About-Cheraw-Town-History-Dizzy-Gillespie-in-Cheraw-10.

Vail, Ken. *Dizzy Gillespie: The Bebop Years 1937–1952*. Oxford: The Scarecrow Press, Inc., 2003.